The Fine Art of Politics

Surprises ahead. Join the party.

The Fine Art of Politics

A Humorous Look at One Era's Unforgettable Politicians

Michele Weston Relkin

SUNSTONE
PRESS
SANTA FE

Sunstone books may be purchased for educational, business, or sales promotional use.
For information please write: Special Markets Department, Sunstone Press,
P.O. Box 2321, Santa Fe, New Mexico 87504-2321.

Book and cover design › L.R. Ahl
Printed on acid-free paper
∞

———————————————

Library of Congress Cataloging-in-Publication Data

Names: Relkin, Michele Weston, 1946- artist.
Title: The fine art of politics : a humorous look at one era's unforgettable
    politicians / by Michele Weston Relkin.
Description: Santa Fe, New Mexico : Sunstone Press, 2019.
Identifiers: LCCN 2018057055 | ISBN 9781632932549 (softcover : alk. paper)
Subjects: LCSH: Painting--Humor. | Politicians--United States--Caricatures
    and cartoons. | United States--Politics and
    government--2009-2017--Caricatures and cartoons.
Classification: LCC ND1156 .R45 2019 | DDC 750.102/07--dc23
LC record available at https://lccn.loc.gov/2018057055

———————————————

WWW.SUNSTONEPRESS.COM
SUNSTONE PRESS / POST OFFICE BOX 2321 / SANTA FE, NM 87504-2321 /USA
(505) 988-4418 / ORDERS ONLY (800) 243-5644 / FAX (505) 988-1025

Guess who I am?

I do not side politically with my artwork but try to bring a smile that is nonpartisan.

—*Michele Weston Relkin*

The Luncheon
of the Boating Party
by *Pierre Auguste Renoir*

8

Hillary Clinton, Donald Trump, Ted Cruz,
Bernie Sanders, Chris Christie, Carly Fiorina

In the Circus: The Ring Master

by *Henri de Toulouse Lautrec*

11

Hillary Clinton

12

Henry VIII
by *Hans Holbein the Younger*

Donald Trump

The Juggler
by *Marc Chagall*

Rand Paul

The Peaceable Kingdom

by *Edward Hicks*

Hillary Clinton, Donald Trump, Ted Cruz,
Bernie Sanders, Chris Christie, Ben Carson,
Jim Gilmore, Bobby Jindal, Jeb Bush,
John Kasich, Andy Martin, George Pataki

The Old Guitarist

by *Pablo Picasso*

16

Bernie Sanders

Detail from a Mural

by *Tommaso di Cristoforo*

Jim Gilmore

Detail from a Mural

by *Tommaso di Cristoforo*

Ben Carson

Stag at Sharkey's

by *George Bellows*

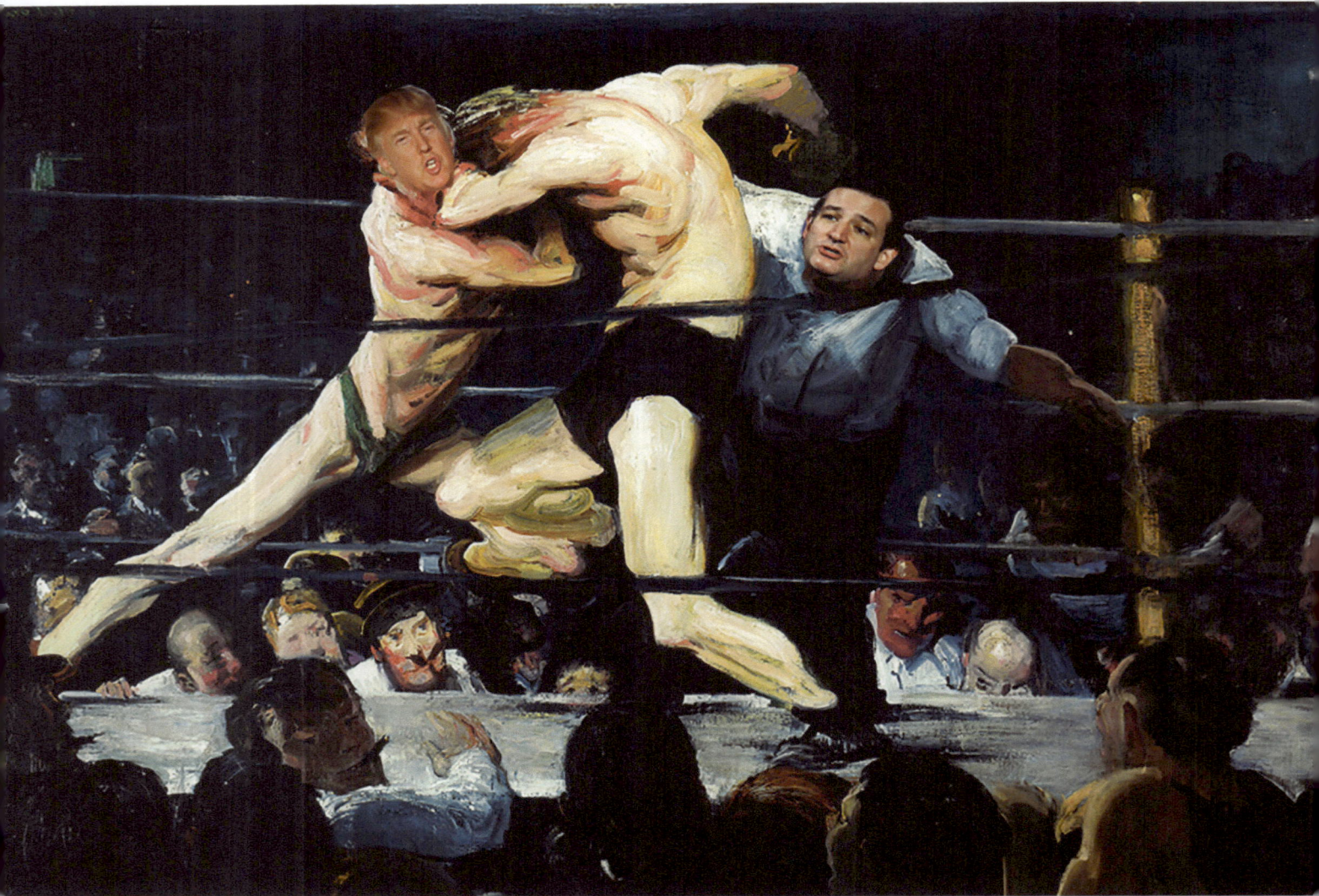

Donald Trump, Ted Cruz

Pierrot

by *Pablo Picasso*

Martin O'Malley

The Marriage of Giovannie Arnolfini and Giovanna Cenami

by *Jan Van Eyck*

Hillary and Bill Clinton

The Ship of Fools

by *Hieronymus Bosch*

23

Hillary Clinton
Chris Christie
Jim Gilmore
Bobby Jindal
George Pataki
Rick Santorum
Lindsey Graham

White Plumes
by *Henri Matisse*

Carly Fiorina

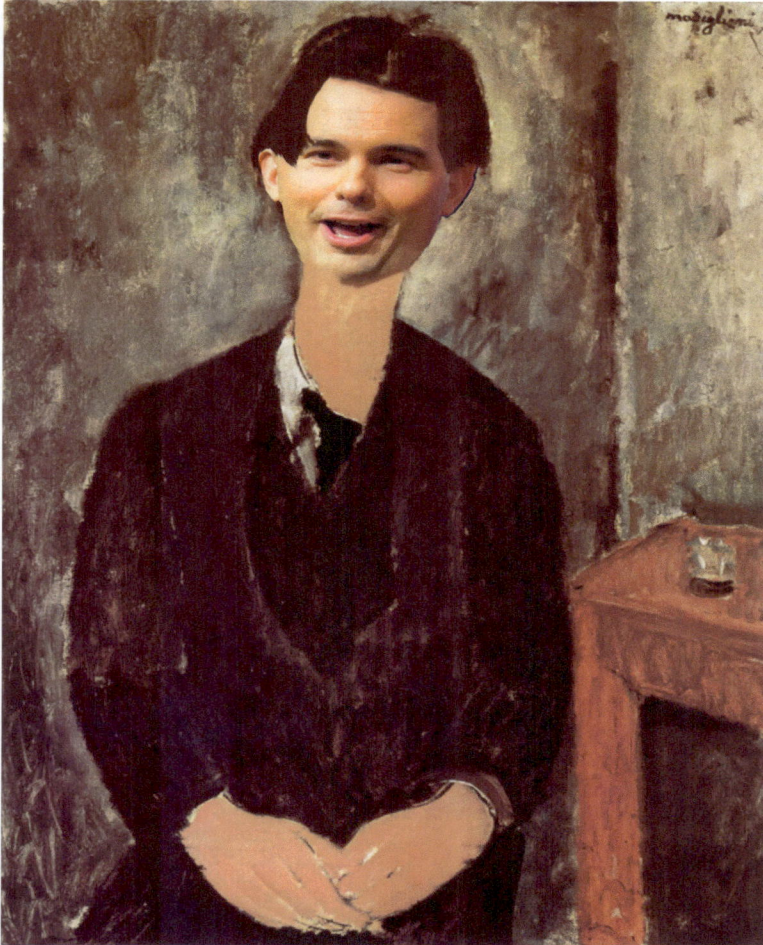

Chaim Soutine
by *Amedeo Modigliani*

Scott Walker

A Couple in a Sailing Boat

by *Edouard Manet*

27

Carly Fiorina, Marco Rubio

Perseus
Freeing
Andromeda

by *Piero di Cosimo*

28

Hillary Clinton,
Donald Trump

Prince Edward, Count Palatine of Simmern

by *Gerrit Van Honthorst*

Donald Trump

The Sleeping Gypsy

by *Henri Rousseau*

30

Ben Carson

The Three Favorite Aerial Travellers

by *John Francis Rigaud*

Hillary Clinton, Donald Trump, Marco Rubio

Boy in a Red Vest

by *Paul Cezanne*

Bobby Jindal

The Maids of Honor
by *Diego Velzquez*

Hillary Clinton, Donald Trump, Marco Rubio, Bernie Sanders, Ben Carson, Jim Gilmore, Ted Cruz, Jeb Bush

As the Old Sing, So the Young Pipe

by *Jacob Jordaens*

Hillary Clinton, Bernie Sanders,
Bill Clinton, Donald Trump, Marco Rubio,
Martin O'Malley, Chris Christie,
Carly Fiorina

The Young Sailor II

by *Henri Matisse*

George Pataki

The Passion of Sacco and Vanzetti

by *Ben Shahn*

Rand Paul, Andy Martin, Rick Perry

Three Musicians

by *Pablo Picasso*

Jeb Bush, Mike Huckabee,
Rand Paul

American Gothic
by *Grant Wood*

Hillary Clinton, Donald Trump

Two Nudes

by *Pablo Picasso*

Hillary Clinton, Carly Fiorina

The Land of Cockaigne

by *Pieter van der Heyden*

Jeb Bush, Ted Cruz, Chris Christie

The Winning Hand
by *Georges Croegaert*

47

Hillary Clinton, Donald Trump

If we shadows have offended,
Think but this, and all is mended,
That you have but slumbered here
While these visions did appear.

—*William Shakespeare*

About the Artist

Michele Weston Relkin is one of Santa Fe, New Mexico's best known living and working artists. She became famous for her social realistic paintings that have occupied the White House for many years. Her work explores many depths outside this venue including mythological, figurative and visual landscapes.

She is the creator of "Inside-Out," a rich celebration of her students' work. Michele teaches and encourages all her students to greater levels of accomplishments through her private and group workshops. Her paintings are enjoyed throughout the United States and Europe.

(Can you find her in the painting across the page?)

The Straw Manikin

by *Francisco Goya*

Michele Weston Relkin